PRAISE FOR THE FALKLAND QUARTET AND OTHER POEMS

"Whedon's meditations range from the nature of romantic love and familial kinship; to the effects of weather, landscape, and Darwinian isolation on our human species; to the tensions between a brightly lit past and a diminishing present. And whatever the mood — plaintive, desolate, drunkenly amorous, or chaotically comedic — Whedon's linguistic dexterity, his mix of tones and dictions, and the freshness and nonlinearity of his storytelling, light up these tales of hardship and heartache breathing them to life in the best of epic traditions."
—Neil Shepard, author of *Vermont Exit Ramps*

"The worth of sons, daughters, husbands, wives, grandparents, caught up in dramas where you wouldn't think of them happening, the connections are many and the words are a brilliant weaving of beauty, craziness, regret, and sadness. There is humor and joy but, mixed with booze, anger or violence, it is suspect. Each page puts us in the middle of another world, hemisphere, time, even gender. These are masterful pieces that won't go quietly into categories, but only into our appreciation for the imagination from which they came."
—Tom Fay, jazz pianist (Gerry Mulligan band) & composer

"What strange, insistent, inescapable poems, these poems by Tony Whedon, of hard love and hard life's filthy luck in a cold, seacoast country's shattered mirror of reality, brilliant as brine, laced inevitably with human pluck and bad luck. I've never read a book of poems like this, as confident and arrogant in their collective impact as a novel. The strangeness of its voice is oceanic, at once heavy and blithe, tides advancing and crashing, or receding and exposing the stench and decomposition that lies in the muck beneath the otherwise gorgeous, restlessly muscular, sapphire sea."
—Kenneth Rosen, author of *The Origins of Tragedy*

The Falkland Quartet and Other Poems

Tony Whedon

with paintings by Morgan O'Connell

Fomite
Burlington, VT

© Poems copyright 2014 – Tony Whedon
   Paintings copyright 2014 – Morgan O'Connell

All rights reserved. No part of this book may be reproduced in any form or by any means without the prior written consent of the publisher, except in the case of brief quotations used in reviews and certain other noncommercial uses permitted by copyright law.

This is a work of fiction. Names, characters and incidents are either the product of the author's imagination or are used fictitiously. Any resemblance to actual persons, living or dead, is entirely coincidental.

ISBN-13: 978-1-937677-76-3
Library of Congress Control Number: 2014948688

Fomite
58 Peru Street
Burlington, VT 05401
www.fomitepress.com

Cover Painting – *South Beach Wave #1* Morgan O'Connell

Contents

Part One

The Falkland Quartet   3

Part Two

I.
Equinox	31
Brothers in Crime	32
Early October Snow	33
Suicide Uncle	35
At St. Isidore's	36
Dutchman	38
For Gramps	39
Target Practice	41
What the Body Does	42
Bee Keeper	43
Parade	44
Amber, Amethyst & Mylar	45
Handcuffs	47
The *Cutlass*	48
Haggard	49

II.
Castaways	50
At Lyme	59
At Biff's Donuts,	60
Pastoral	62
Local Color	63
Reach	67
Dockside	68
Hunger	70
Portrait	73
Ferris' Wheel of History	74
Still Life	77
Doomed Love	79
Turtle	80
Sanctuary	82
Aubade	83
The Winter Journal	84

Part One

The Falkland Quartet

"*On March 1st, 1833, and again on March 16th, 1834, the Beagle anchored in Berkeley Sound, in East Falkland Island. This archipelago is situated in nearly the same latitude with the mouth of the Strait of Magellan; it covers a space of one hundred and twenty by sixty geographical miles, and is a little more than half the size of Ireland. After the possession of these miserable islands had been contested by France, Spain and England, they were left uninhabited. The government of Buenos Ayres then sold them to a private individual, but likewise used them, as old Spain had done before, for a penal settlement. England claimed her right and seized them. The Englishman who was left in charge of the flag was consequently murdered. A British officer was then sent unsupported by any power: and when we arrived, we found him in charge of a population, of which rather more than half were runaway rebels and murderers. . ."*

– Charles Darwin, *The Voyage of the Beagle*

I.

Begin in an airport – a bald botanist

with his entomologist wife,
      a week past Easter, Month of the Comet,
Hair of the Dog, years since
      I wrote a line – so please forgive
if my vision's opaque, the scenery a little damp:

Peg's misplaced our passports
      and rifles through a cosmetics bag
to find our royal blue Canadian visas
      smeared with toothpaste, mascara.
Outside a muted April rain.

We switch planes in muggy Miami.
          Beyond the jetstream trades,
south & east, past Brazil, the Guianas,
          due east across the South Atlantic
over Ascension

then sou'west – the sea a sunset pink –
          into the grief-soaked roaring 'forties
we swoop toward autumnal
          Port Stanley. A week after Easter, smoke
churns from Granma Edna's chimney.

Greeting my wife, Edna's amazed at her little girl's
          plump warmth. The old woman stands
in a kitchen that gives onto
          a garden alive with thyme & stunted marigolds;
a picket fence rebukes the South Atlantic:

ducks splash in a bomb crater. Among
          stones & gorse cartridges litter the beach
like cockleshells. This is home to you, says Edna,
          showing me rootcellar & pantry,
a staircase climbing to the captain's walk

from where we spot sporting seals, shelfrock
          heaped with teeming sealife, &– phantomed
by ceaseless spray – the prow of
          a barnacled British frigate.
Late at night, Peggy & Edna asleep,

I gaze out at moonlit gun placements,
          happy because Peggy's home again –
the war years over, teals nesting in
          oxidizing jeeps & spent howitzer shells.
On his deathbed Peggy's disillusioned father

called the islands "Fuckland." She left here
          at the start of the war – quick
& pretty with buck Falkland teeth
          (a dentist in Halifax straightened them)
and a "kelper's" mistrust of authority.

Her dad, a pudgy Scots, imported wool
        to the Maritimes; her mother (dead now)
played cribbage with Halifax's
        Ladies Auxillary. Peggy & I met at Dalhousie
in Marine Biology over petri-dished

Bay of Fundy scum: I recall more
        the blurr of amoebas,
the obscenely swirling paramecia,
        than I do Peggy's freckled face.
We fell in love over my tattered "Howl,"

saw Ginzberg once chanting poems
        at a save-the-whales symposium;
she liked the unbuttoned beat of his lines,
        but her loyalties lay (still lie)
with Ahab, whalers & the whaling life.

In Halifax her dad outfitted trawlers,
        joined the Masons, taught Sunday school
& formed a club of expat "kelpers" who
        kept the faith over pots of imported rye.
Peggy's first of the family back –

she's more in culture shock than I,
        if you call *her* amazement at
Grandma's homely hovel "shock": we're socked in
        next morning by a so'wester. Flakes splat
against the windows; a gale leaks in

through wall cracks, the roof buckles
        in the storm. When we go walking it's enough
to stay upright. Halfway to Smuggler's Cove
        the wind stops & across the grass
spots of Fall sunlight dazzle us.

"Always it's like this," Peggy sniffs: "Fickle.
        All year a big low pressure cell squats
& pisses over the Falklands. Cold air's
        sucked up from the sub Antarctic. Thus,
December snow (our South Atlantic summer):

you've noticed no trees grow here."
        We're looking north under slate clouds
toward a blotch of frothy nothing.
        "If there was a sunny day they called off school.
My playmates were two plump Toulouse geese –."

We lunge through the grass to a pillbox
        dug into muddy hillside: a gun turret
surveys the milky firth, the quonset huts
        & bunkers of RAF garrisons hunkered
outside Port Stanley. It's all flinty,

Moorish, Bronteesque. Inside the pillbox
        there's scattered tins, neatly piled
British rubbish: a copy of all things –
        Adam Bede – pages yellowed,
& a marbled notebook with poems

in a schoolboy hand:

  "They tell us the spics are scum –
and I think they're right, by gum."

Unaccountably, Peggy's weeping. "Take
        the flightless Steamer Duck," she says:
"It ought to dream of flight, but from where to what?
        Nothing to fear here but old age & death.
Or boredom – impossible if you're a duck."

Peggy spent a girlhood collecting gulls' eggs
        & the rare Falkland fritillary butterfly;
she hammered out Bach on a tuneless
        church spinet: I see her squinting
in Port Stanley's dim library and think

of the flights the mind makes
        to escape the Imagination's muck.
If you're a duck, nights you bob, halfasleep,
        in lush marsh grass, dreaming your wings work;
if you're Peggy, you plan escape.

Stowed-away in the fuselage
        of the twice-weekly
cargo plane from Montevideo.
        "I never owned a watch," she says. "The days oozed by,
hour after hour." Her games of make-believe

included "storm the castle."
        Her imaginary friend, a Venusian droid,
saved Peggy from marriage to this
        or that shepherd or trawler steward
or guano gatherer. Steamer ducks sit squat

on the water. One of a kind,
        they're a species Darwin spied
in the tidal guts he moored in:
        sans predators & awkwardly buoyant, they marked
the perimeter of what was already

a bustling Port Stanley harbor.
        From the *Beagle* Darwin would've spied
roaring sea lions stacked like cord wood
        (a hundred thousand more than today)
on the outer islets, teeming, prolific,

but ultimately almost "dodo'd"
        along with puffins & passenger pigeons.

II.

Back at Grandma's we watch
evening rise up across the firth.

Peggy sets out teacozies, crumpets,
and Edna tunes in the BBC & falls asleep;

then, quickly, Peggy at just past eight o'clock.
Next morning Edna maps out our visit

to the family grave; I'm in the sitting room,
dogeared British poetry anthology on my lap,

Hopkin's kelly meadows, Wordsworth's bowers,
mintgreen in the blousy lower latitudes,

graveyard poems & abbeys in the misty funk.
As Edna warbles from the kitchen

I see stashed on her shelf among
the Conan Doyles, nautical charts,

stacks of postcards (Scotland – the Hebrides),
a disintegrating family bible (Gideon)

& assorted Classics (Marcus Aurelius,
and odd volumes of Catallus & Ovid).

Edna announces we'll pack lunches, bring mums,
have tea with Peg's relatives. Old Mr. Dart,

Edna's neighbor, arrives in his roofless Land Rover.
Retired from the Argentine, Dart's demeanor's

churlish: we're off in puffs of exhaust
(stentorian hack of rusty muffler),

sheepskin rugs across our laps,
following jeep ruts along the island's spine,

all windswept, green & wonderful – until
the Rover's engine sputters & goes dead.

Dart bangs his wrench on the steaming block;
miles from Goose Greene, the weather's putrid.

So what better place to have our lunch?
Peggy says. (Dart's not optimistic.)

Edna sets out boiled eggs & biscuits beneath
a makeshift tarp. We eat as bevies of teal skirl

& wheel in gusty updrafts: it's all breezy flutter –
tarp flapping, a disgruntled Dart

flinging himself at the windswept Rover. There's
time enough to rummage through the gorse

to see if more than weeds abide here. Stones
slathered with moss & Antarctic lichen;

leathery leafed bear berries (the fruit less
than delicious) but little more to catch

my eye till I spy a lady slipper,
its minute hairs a shield against the wind.

All of which reminds me how hard
it is for Edna & Dart to live here. There's

nothing to do, Dart says, but hoof it down
the road to Goose Green. "Twenty miles," cries Edna –

"that's twenty miles!" But it's muck & trudge
through fens, across moors, Edna's mossy hair

gone crazy in the wind, her face pale,
breath coming fast. Unaccountably,

I find myself liking sad daunted Dart,
blemishes & all. As we walk he monologues us

with stories of sheep-filled nights,
sour smell of tanning leather –

how he arrived from London in Buenos Aires,
exiled from a bad marriage:

of Peronista politics, botched business deals,
abortive coups – and finally

a trip south – "my tanneries took me
to the Pampas where I lived ten sad years,

the only Scot in that loutish Kraut crowd.
Then at the ripe age of sixty I met Dot –

Been married to a *gaucho*. We honeymooned
in Tierra del Fuego. I gave up

the leather export business,
took up the tango." The road unthreads

below us. Edna's pekid;
Peggy's sniffly – but Dart's got

his second wind: there were five years with Dot.
"We'd saddle up Tuesdays, she and I, & ride

our ponies to where the Andes rose up like
tawny teeth & cattle land gave way to arroyos;

condors soared, the rare Patagonian
lark poured out its heart." Dart wipes a tear, sighs,

sits on a boulder. The beach below spits & fumes.
Beyond the breakers a British sub surfaces

& rolls slightly starboard, sinister, black.
"Then came the bad years. Dot's family were liberals;

her daughter became a *desparecido* –
of course we lived in terror – Dot

shut up herself alone in our attic.'"
On the road now, Peggy takes the lead –

a fuming sky hurls down snowy epithets – & as
we walk Dart picks up his tale where

he left off: Dot dead, the dictatorship
in full stride. The generals cut inflation;

capitalism ran rampant; a cabal
of defrocked Gestapo installed *Auf Deutsche*

in public schools. Meanwhile a languishing Dart
lost himself in reveries of Dot,

the schoolgirl magic of her tinseled laughter.
Wind at our backs, down the cratered road,

twelve clicks to Goose Greene, a faint sulfur smell
wafts across the flats: a few errant penguins

waddle up the shingle – a flock of glad-handing
tuxedo'd tipplers on the march to nowhere.

Night in Aunt Sal's transplanted English cottage,
I listen to the sea roar: what difference

if only Dart mourns? On the island's edge,
there's just patches of bleak stone houses huddled

against the storm, no sigh of branches,
shifting house timbers, thunder of the South Atlantic,

the grand blanching shimmer of stars. "It's
not the same," says Peggy, squinching close.

"Our little family – not a man around. Maybe
I shouldn't've come back – it's

more than desolate, it's godforsaken.
I don't recall Goose Greene was . . . but then,

who'll explain to you." I brush her hair back;
there's an angry glint in her eyes.

"My father never wanted me married off
the islands. You were – in his cranky way

of seeing things – too effete,
too English, though you'd never

been to England. Sometimes I wonder. . .
how you & I – but there's no need saying what

scares me, you know – don't you? –
the frumpy woman I might've been, like

– God bless her – Grandma Edna."
Her voice trails off. She's lightly snoring.

III

To the north hazy cliffs –
& south the Greene's lights lantern
the cove. Each wave along
the shore's lifted & shot back

a second time. In this seascape –
so cold, so lonely – when I spit
at the stars they almost sizzle,
the sky's a dark near-blue

& the hills beyond the cove
bare the vexing marks of
an exile's vista – rumpled,
rolling up & over a sky stretched

near to infinity. Farther down the beach,
I trip on an eel's carcass. The
dark stench sends me reeling –
but the ocean's indrawn breath, soft

against the shingle, brings me back,
and I lean down, glimpse shimmering
minnows, glittering micro-
organismic clutter. I think

of Peg's words before she fell asleep,
how they trailed off –
half accusation,
half disgust, at herself

for coming back to inevitable ennui,
disappointment – to a return
that's more a revision
of the past than a revisiting,

an exploration of. . . relics –
those moldering hulks –
of Darwinian disaster, and how little
difference this trip makes

in her life's grand scheme. But
then I think it's unnatural & cruel
to put myself in her shoes: tonight
I dream Peg's father's roaring drunk –

that old decrepit half-senile man
back in Goose Greene, leading a clan of
redfaced Highlanders –
they've seized a windy slope:

they wheeze out an air, then the hill's a whale shape –
but it's not a whale, though
hugely swollen, & rises
billowing, flickering a moment, then

gone out – but not really gone.
I'd like to think – I need
to believe (skeptically) – our souls
blend & disperse, like these thoughts,

across the sea, but Halifax,
our marriage – this journey into
frigid nothingness . . . we'd thought
a bracing wind would revive and

distract Peggy from her studies,
renew my delight in botany –
but next morning it's all the same.
The planet creaks on its axis. My mind

tumbles into darkness.
Aunt Sal – a cheerless widow just past forty –
serves a breakfast of fritters lathered with
gooseberry jam. Sal hasn't seen Peggy

since the early 'eighties,
& what she recalls is shy, bookish,
a loose limbed, curious child who spent summers –
what passes for summers,

those tart brief sub-Antarctic summers –
poring over biology books or rambling
the rookeries below Sal's cottage.
Sal – herself "literary" –

has frayed *Geographics* on shelves
cluttered with shells & weathered stones
& whisky bottles.
She smokes corktipped Dunhills, refers

longingly to a trip to France
before the Falklands War,
recalls the bistros & bookstalls,
the jubilant student barricades

of poststructuralist Paris. "But all that's
lost to me now. Since Wilfried fell
from Mount Usborne – in an icestorm –
I've been salted away in Goose Greene."

"The Greene's precious little secret."
Dart grins."Mr. Dart's an incorrigible flirt,"
Sal says. "And how are you Edna?"
she turns to Grandma, pale & shivering

beneath a shawl. "Afraid not so well,"
Edna nods toward. . .
she's about to exit into eternity.
The women rustle through scrapbooks,

sighing over snaps of island life before
two thousand Brits descended –
parchesi, quilting bees;
Presbyterian rummage sales,

shearing tournaments,
drab sunrises, & marathon naps
on winter afternoons. "I miss the peace,
the quiet," declares Dart: "Now the weather's wicked."

"Dear Dart, it's always wicked," Sal says.
"I miss the whaling days. Blubber soap,
sperm whale oil," Edna reminisces.
"And astringent whale soap.

The right soap from the Right Whale." Sal
clears our plates & looks at Peggy who,
if she recalls anything, won't divulge –
or even digress to life with me

in our Halifax house;
it's a matter of attitude – or latitude –
these differences that erupt
in disjunct geographies, or so thinks Peggy

who's brought a microscope to
inspect the island's lichen.
I want no more than a little sun in my face,
a walk on a bouldery beach,

or to sit, Peggy's head in my lap,
gazing at galaxies. Almost noon the weather
clears. Clouds stucco the hills.
Sal talks earnestly of her life with Wilfried,

the day the exiled Dutch diplomat
arrived in his beatup yawl, "The Dice,"
jib and mainsail ripped by williwas
in wild, unpronounceable places.

"I knew," she says. "He was gallantly,
unabashedly, rich. He sailed out of
of Curacao & Suriname,
made his living trading on a modest

mythomania. An abortive try at
the Straits of Magellan
forced him to limp east past Ascension
& the Sandwiches – where he put in for

provisions – & then north
through the gale,
trailed by an obligatory albatross,
to plain, prim Port Stanley."

Sal describes Wilfried's
chiseled chin; his aquatic eyes
whose gaze taught her that night
aboard his yacht to say,

"I Want You" in Dutch, Mandarin & Portuguese.
"His skin was an unwrinkled,
Indonesian olive – betraying
his mother's Sumatran origins –

but those eyes were Delft blue.
A nautical Vermeer blue." Sal pauses,
lights her Dunhill. "He'd spent the postwar years
trading trinkets in steamy Suriname:

became an honorary Maroon,
or so he said; rumor in Port Stanley had it
dear Wilfried was on the lam from
authorities in the Netherlands.

I don't know if loving him meant
I believed in him – but I did.
And those stories –Wilfred had yarns
about waterspouts, ghost ships,

& mutiny that kept me amused, awake –
& I can't tell you how much I loved to be with him –
each night a new promenade, a new perfume –
& I loved the scent of him –

the gats & sewers of Bombay,
the gumbos, the soufles of dusty Cayenne.
But my lover had fits & rages. He
sulked. He pouted. He loved our low Dutch sky,

our life on the world's bum. He was fond
of island junk, Falkland bric-a-brac:
rusty harpoons, paintchipped figureheads
from beached schooners. . . He liked all that."

We follow Sal outside to her garden –
like Edna's, weedless & prissy, looking down
on acres of marsh. Unlike Edna's,
Sal's plot's rife with exotics:

purple kohlrabi, New Zealand spinach,
wind-blistered ornamental cabbage.
"I've devoted my life to making things grow here:
Wil thought it foolish – but he was fond

of tulips, which did survive – mail-order
Rotterdam bulbs – perky as penguins."

IV.

Then – gusts of wind –
limpid rain – & inside again,
Sal retrieves Wil's journal

& my mind wanders: I see in the Falklands'
krill-filled waters a port for misfits,
malcontents – a colony, a bilious crowd

of probably pirates:
"*The theatre is worthy of the scene
acted on it,*" says Darwin.

"*An undulating land,
with a desolate and wretched
aspect.*" But what interests me

are those demi-scenes, lit within
by the humming halflives
of minds tortured by a Fate

leaving them here centuries before:
it now attracts others
equally unfortunate. "*. . .everywhere,*"

Darwin goes on, "*. . . a peaty soil,
and wiry grass, of one monotonous
brown color. Here and there

a peak or ridge of grey quartz
rock breaks through the smooth
surface.*" Reading the Beagle journals

I can't fault the man
with lack of imagination, though
I'd have liked less about

the pampas *gauchos* he brought
with him and more on those *"runaway
rebels and murderers"*

from whom Peggy descends on
her mother's side – and with whom
Sal's Wilfried would have

empathized. Wilfried's journal
reveals a man obsessed
more with his own health

than with a romance worthy
of Sal's Wagnerian conception of him:
"'We lie at anchor three days," she reads.

"Feel sick. South Atlantic sun
at its nadir – my complexion rancid;
I've searched out Port Stanley

apothecaries but nothing helps,
calves swell, ankles blister.
Amuse myself with a Dutch thriller

– set in a dingy prewar Antwerp;
meet Sal in the Port Stanley library.'
Truth is, I'd had a conversion

the year before," Sal says.
"In my cousin's trawler.
Among the smelt & flounder

I kneel down, say the Lord's Prayer –
still a Godfearing Presbyterian.
Once, actually, I saw a mermaid.

She was rather plain, oddly freckled,
shivering on a dock piling,
& what struck me, of course,

was how bloody cold she was.
But about my conversion – Peggy
must understand, I'm sure Edna does,

how the mind works here; how
the lack of light tricks you into a belief
in higher orders. Either

you're drenched in awe or bone dry.
Our shepherds & fisher folk,
accustomed to random death, splendid

isolation, are literate as Icelanders.
(Some say we're inbred.)
I knew your wife from Goose Greene visits

when she was a child: I see her sulking
in the library stacks, leafing through
Nature journals. I studied theology

actually at the U of Wales – wish
I'd done the natural sciences,
like you, Peggy." "Well – I, like you,"

Peggy says, "was thrown back on my own devices.
Lost in the estuaries, the tidal tarns
& guts – or out on a reach in my father's catboat;

I loved to sail. But I've no philosophical
inclination – I just don't know
what to do with ideas. That's

what separates me from my husband.
I thought I'd like coming home,
returning to the real, the tangible –

suction cups on star fish, a seasick snail. . .
– but it's all strange to me."
We scramble up. . . to a graveyard,

headstones weathered with
epitaphs for the unburied dead,
water widows awaiting ships long overdue.

Peggy's family's in back, a plot
that thickens to cattails, rushes, and
from a tumbling wall we gaze down

at Goose Greene's stone houses, each
facing its own ruined future.
Edna mumbles a prayer

for her husband – "He ran a cutter
between the west & east islands,"
she manages, "lost his bearings & went up

on the shoals. Never found the fellow" –
and she stoops down,
scoops up handfuls of pebbles,

murmuring, & tosses them far & wide,
a ritual Peggy repeats for her father
buried beneath Nova Scotia sod

as does Sal for Wilfried –
his tombstone glowers above the rest –
not a sweet moment, bitterness all around,

dreams six feet under,
wind too raw, too wild, for elegy,
a sky too gray, & our mood so sullen

we forget ourselves, each of us
on his own descent – this time
along the island's grassy thigh –

& a kind of sweet dissembling overtakes us,
we're shades mumbling, dissimulating – "I loved him. . .
she loved me" – even as we descend.

* *

It's back to Halifax,
at an ungodly five AM,

Peggy ragged and out-of-of-sorts,
and me down with the three-day Falkland crud.

(Lord, please save us from ourselves) & thence
at sunup to our waterside cottage,

our fat Tom snaking between my legs,
too grateful to purr, & a reek of cat piss,

roof leak from a Nor'easter that came
and went while we were gone. The bed sheets

are ungodly damp. I spoon with Peggy
and try to snatch a wink, but can't.

The alarm clock ticking, the cat at our feet
kneading himself to sleep. Latitudinal jetlag,

they call it. Antipodal anomie, one equinox
displacing another & the mind a swamp

of *what ifs* as I pour my third cup of coffee.
Sweet the wind raking the willows,

and bittersweet Sal's voice on Tuesday
cheering us off to Halifax. A trot to the mailbox

proves tonic. Then sunlight & mist,
privet hedge and blessed dogwood bursting

on the road. Back from the world's bum
the quotidian lurches up to greet me:

the mailbox is chockfull of this & that,
and my life seems quite ordinary.

Peggy's up when I get back. She sorts
the junk mail to find a letter, postmarked

"Haggard," from my brother David I've not seen
since Mum's funeral ten years back. He chose

a "road less traveled," not that we didn't get along,
but a thread of love unraveled between us after

he took up with Ellie & sailed to Cuba, like our dad
did years ago. Fingers atremble, I slit

open the letter. Peggy's not functioning –
caught in vertigo from our equatorial transit,

she can't hear me cry out as I read:
"Been an accident" (with no salutation).

"Ellie killed on the shore road from Pubnico to Halifax,
dead on impact & not breathing. I can't forget –

do you understand ? - - the shattered glass and
twirling headlights, the Portuguese couple with

a yipping dog who found her. Hours later, I'm there,
and *not* there, Skid marks and an ungodly quiet

mark the scene. Her car's gutted carcass declares:

          THIS HAPPENED

then the bell toll & harbor lights through streaming fog;
Ellie's body like a burst placenta, the culpable Pontiac

and sweet Prince Edward deer (guiltily grazing.)
The smashed, purpled maple and "B"movie clouds.

The shadowy tidal pools and her heart held
by an invisible cord to her body." That's all

I'll transcribe here. I await a plea – a cry – for cash,
a place to crash, and thankfully that never comes.

He's shipped out on a trawler. Off the Outer Banks,
one more in a line of David's broken lives begins.

Peggy says I'm optimistic. Truth is nothing's to be done.
"The night lasts and lasts," she says, wiping tears from my chin

"A few more gruesome hours before dawn."

Part Two

I

Equinox

I stood outside the goodwill shop
and watched my father
rummage the sailor's socks
& sweaters, his hands shaky
when he held up a ratty vest:
then we rode home and by noon
he was on the phone making notes on a business deal
(used tires) he wouldn't remember sober.
(Between each town he'd rave about his salesmanship,
"I'm the best, the best!") For lunch he boiled
some eggs. Though it was May,
it began snowing big flaky flakes
pretty against the woods and the
huge truck tires. My father had transported
them to our cottage near Halifax
and they were piled in shitty coils
on the cove where the Cuban freighters
would pick them up. At eleven
in the morning my father
was already drunk. He put one egg
on the table, he explained
how at the equinox it would be perfectly
balanced: over and over,
he tried to make the egg stand upright.
I looked at his hands,
his white cheeks & pocked forehead,
but I didn't want to watch now.
It was raining harder,
breakfast was over & the collie
was scratching at the door.

BROTHERS IN CRIME

After we broke into the bait shop & stole
the lures and fishing line, we drank
the old man's schnapps, one gulp and
it was done. That's me up to
no good and my older brother Chet
out on the breakwater when the tide
comes in. We're fishing like maniacs --
stripers, shad, the works. The town
behind us shrunk to the size of
a blueberry. That's my brother, the scholar.
I'm the dreamy one, three years
behind him, smoking Export A's
and swearing like my old man. Play
this song fast, play it soft. The waves
doing brush work. The bass notes are the wind.

Early October Snow

Used to be you'd welcome a spitty
first snow – little kid humped along,
betrayed by God, Man & Weather – & you'd need
to see the cut under the eyebrow,
the indecent wink, the sweet first frost, to see the bitter
grass & rusty tools tidied up; after the year's
first snow the dog's feet are puddle-crusted;
the sky's all roily and full of signs that say
you are embarked into a time of quiet,
of calm, which is to say, you must shake through
this moment and though you're shaking, you call it calm.
You woke up thirsty this October morning:
along the avenue of crisp beeches it was written
in the jays' wry catcalls, in memory's pneumatic sigh,
how the lungs floated, how the
angry blood rose in the warm false blush of a
life given over. All morning you scrubbed
the cows with a wire brush, made them clean, clean.

Suicide Uncle

When I found a photo of Uncle Dave
I knew who he was – the flattened lips,

the bottlegray eyes – standing in front of
a beach fraught with perfect little waves.

My "suicide uncle" I always call him
whose body they discovered by a turn in the river.

There were gambling debts, a black lab
who mourned him ferociously.

The story picks up after Dave's death.
The photo shows my uncle grinning

his Newfy grin – is he puzzled or
or just disinterested? Out of some gristle of

ambition & some priceless yearning for *what*
my uncle inserted the Remington

into his mouth & blew his brains out.
I call him a fortunate accident – I've

so much to learn from his death
about sudden impulses, sudden regrets.

Who knows what in hell he was doing alive.

At St. Isidore's

I sat in the old windmill with my grandfather
that late September noon & watched him
at the pulleys & gears for the last time.
He was going away & so was I: the leaves

on the cottonwood went silvery in the wind
& the wheel began to turn. Creak, creak.
But there was nothing I could do – Gramps
was heading to rainy St. Johns

& next morning I'd ride the bus north
for my year among the Jesuits.
If Gramps helped me love & forget,
the Brothers of the Cross made me remember.

The school sat high on a promontory,
the Bay of Fundy stretching out past
quarreling gulls & rocks. Hate
isn't the right word for what I felt for St. Isidore's –

each of us boys had his own little horror story.
The worst part was I began to like the icy showers,
the iron discipline. Once I banged my head
on the threshold to the confessional –

the blood spurted, I couldn't forgive myself for that.
I hated the cod breakfasts, the ritual calluses,
& I prayed gramps would rescue me. After Matins
I'd find myself looking through the dorm window

onto the cobblestones, the lights in the church blinking out
& I'd tell myself I had to learn patience. Gramps died
in St. Johns that April – & to mark his death
I read to myself the Gospel of Luke, not the way

the Brothers would have me read it – revenge
& the devil's mayhem on my lips – but under the light
of an Easter moon; and when I closed my eyes,
all I saw was the great orb of the windmill, turning, turning.

DUTCHMAN

The gale was still going on & big combers raked
the shore. The old man was deeply rattled.
"Our Father who Art in Hell, Shit Faced be your name,"
Chet joked when our father died. We were that used
to him being plastered. Beyond the harbor The *Dutchman*
labored through deep green troughs to shore.
My brother bet she wouldn't make it & in the bitter
end we split the difference. He's up late, stooped
over a box of sphagnum moss, their tiny tendrils
reaching up to heaven. The old man died one hellish
night in January. Six months till Spring & the ground
froze six feet under. That's The *Dutchman*,
the busted remains of her, ten years later,
gone to her grave on the Grand Banks bottom.

For Gramps

Beyond him, the black-and-white gelded bull
plowing through sun-chokes

as the tree gave and fell,

collapsing

a halfacre of maple saplings,
the ground also giving out

an emphatic whomp, Gramps still leaning
to

where the tree had been, the chainsaw
sputtering

as he jabbed the saw's blade into the split
that went the gnarled length of trunk

to the pealing crotch,
the light sift of snow
fuzzing distance between him and me,

and he said, "That's what made her spin,"
and showed the rift

inside of which white grubs
uncurled in a shock of daylight,

the black maple bole turning to fine humus,
as he breathed more easily

and showed me how to buck the maple
and drag the slash

smiling to the ravine
from where I could see, below, first snow

had covered the logs in the misty clearing.

Target Practice

In the basement my father had a target range.
Ducks he'd shoot at made of tin: he'd pop
the tin ducks & when he'd finished I dug around for what?
Spent shells, smashed Labatt bottles. Though
I was only ten, I wanted the teapots, the doilies.
I wanted the chipped China, the monogrammed
baby spoons, the pearlhandled stuff. I wanted a safe box
with blue lingerie in it. I gave up digging when
the drainpipe broke and I felt the water puddle
around my ankles. It grew darker as we dug & one spared
the other; one breathed when the other breathed
and the smoke rose from my illegal cigarette;
but I never forgot the pick & shovel, the stink of earth,
the cool coal dust. You never get rid of this.
Years later, when you made love to me, I'd forget
the outhouse fragrance, the shovelfuls of mud, the
dead cartridges. We'd stop at a Mom & Pop where
the clams sat rotting in their baskets. Salmon
were climbing a ladder, the rapids ran fresh & rich
with oceans of pink salmon. The truth is I had a history:
I stood facing a river thick with leaping, dying fish –
A girl in a print dress licking a creamy freeze
looking into a smudged window at multiples of me.

What the Body Does

We're all at our worst – Bryce's mom, Ellie, and me,
grieving, like they say, the only way we know:
this Flintstone stoning that Flintstone,
clouds stacked like B52's above the little town.
Bryce's almost gone – the bed's empty, a crystal mobile twirls
above his pillow. Some days, I want to say,
are better than others. "Your mother's loss," Ellie says
and pours a sherry, leans toward the halfopened fridge,
"has nothing to do with loss." And she's right
in her way. We hover around our Dying Bryce – one helluva
preacher – & envy his Baptist upbringing;
we hear birds – nuthatches, phoebes – we never heard before.
Ellie's in the backyard, crying her heart out.
I hear the lab's insistent yapping, the ting of china,
the clinking snifters. Someone coughs, someone talks
mushy. I step onto the dock to drink in the light, dust
drifting, a scent of mahogany. Bryce's mother, dead
drunk, skulks into the basement, & time slows down.
Now I want to say, look we could take this differently,
like the body's folded, it's all grown up
& grown out. I could tell you, help you if you wanted.

BEE KEEPER

Pity me, pity my niece Nardel, pity Clyde
(I can't) & pity the bear with his
mouthful of bees. I remember the

hawthorn porch, the toppled hives
where the bear got in and ate the brood –
the swatches of bear hair, the clawmarks

on Clyde's beebox. The bees swirled,
the sky went black as we sat
on Clydes's porch, watching him

change the oil in his ATV.
He'd gone funny from six months on Elsemere:
home from the Arctic, he took care of my aunt's

five-year old of a previous union. Once
I saw Clyde smack little Nardel
– she'd drunk his brain medicine –

& he sobbed all the way to St. William.
Nardel was at peace & tranquil.
And while we drove, Clyde crossed himself.

Forget the stomach pump,
he cried; I like her sleepy like that.
He didn't want to lose Nardel

like he'd lost his bees. But once Clyde
tried sex with me (Nardel was snoozing
in the boathouse) & as he undid his belt

& commenced to bumble me, Clyde's bees
stung his sly New Brunswick ass.

Parade

Boom, I left Biff in my sixth month.
& I wish I could say I found Jesus.
Dad had worked in a foundry
melting slag into little chunks,
and that's the way it felt –
my legs. One day, a parade.
Fire trucks with crepe on them.
Kids in rain hats, the cannery crew,
the houseboat porches wet
with September rain. I began to feel holy.
I began to be sick late in the afternoon.
I remember we took a ferry to New Brunswick
when I was eight. A freshening wind slopped
the blunt-nosed boats. My father
stood outside the car with my brother
whose real name was Sin. Sin said
he'd stay on deck & watch the girls
from Camp St. Agnes. I remember
them in their army boots,
their red campfire scarves
clanking with girlscout tin.
In a way, I wish I could be eight again,
I wish I were plump with merry
Christian forgiveness. When the ferry
plowed into the barge I watched
the St. Agnes girls fall,
their rose petal scarves floating above them:
Sin jumped in to save them. Sin
dived in the same as I wish I could have.
After Biff & I split up I moved
in with David, a changing of the guard,
& I tried to tell him about my brother,
about the New Brunswick ferry
and my father's hands pumping Sin's chest
til he breathed him back again.

Amber, Amethyst & Mylar

It was a stretch to imagine Rita
pretty, young & tawdry.
She collected rare gems – amethyst, mylar,
little flecks of mica schist – & set them
on the table, fumbling a
lumpy quartz as she told the botched story
of her life. She'd conceived Biff on a whim
in the Canadian Pacific yard,
the smell of jimson burning in the pot-
belly; the railroad dick's trousers heaped
around his ankles. That's how she flat
out said it – waited for it to settle
in. Then she showed me the amber – a dollop
of hardened pine sap with a fly stuck
dead center – & asked if I didn't
want time to stop the way it had
for the fly. If time's got a color,
she said, it's name is Amber. Rita knew
I was pregnant by Biff then; that
if I left her layabout son, time would
rush on, unstoppable. Does this strike
a sympathetic chord? she asked, setting her
little gem box by the window.
I looked at Biff – he was high again
(Rita's rum) – and I said
as much to myself & my unborn baby
as to them I deserved more than
a four-floor walkup, bad teeth & an
early grave. Rita flinched at that
& moments later, she put the bottle
away & stomped into the kitchen. Mom
used to cook sweet Virginia ham
Sundays. Rolling around with candied
carrots & potatoes. She was Greek
but we never ate Greek food – my
father hated it, though the Scotch & Greeks

share a common ancestor. A common
bagpipe. The ham steams on its platter,
the seabirds beat against the wind:
Excuse, I say, and my dad says,
Excused. I don't know why I recall this,
except today I'm watching the lights in
Biff's eyes go out a last last time.
Nothing lasts. And lasts.

Handcuffs

I sat in the police car
watching the river. They
were going to take me
to my mother's and I
was melting all over the
upholstery. Far off
you could hear the sound
of carolers and as we drove up
to the town through banks of snow
firewood was piled
high on front porches
and yellow smoke poured
from the chimneys.
I guess I didn't want to go back –
nothing held me to my home
anymore. Years later
I'd remember how
I got arrested, the
feel of the cuffs
on my wrists. Now, night
drifted over the town:
what was left was after-
light, black buckets
of shade, tarns & guts
& the oily pitch of
tidal flats glittering
like loose money.
I watched the deer
come down through
the dripping branches
& it was off there shining,
that eerie sunset light
draining the memory away.

The *Cutlass*

For six weeks The *Cutlass* sat in the marina,
a ketch cut out for heavy weather, classy with
a Chinese cook. Nights we heard across the water
a tinkle of wine glasses & saucy laughter. Once
we saw her natty captain & a girl dressed in white
out on deck, the portholes splashing pink light
into the harbor. We thought we'd never go farther
than the next little town, never get richer than
our class & station. "No one's goin' nowheres,"
cried Chet, looking out at that floating whorehouse
& a beat-up fishing scow putting into shore.
Our chitchat got grim. I hooked a squid onto my
line & cast into the darkness, a pathetic figure,
waiting for his real life to begin.

Haggard

A month later we holed up across the border in Haggard
waiting for Mother. And I hated it – on principle.
The cabin. The wormy outhouse. The dripping bushes.
One morning my father put on his chemist's gown.

He was planning to blow up Haggard though he had nothing
against the pond where this no place got its name.
He'd been drinking – or he hadn't been; either way,
it was the same – August, the pond turned tealeaf brown

& I missed the kids I'd left in Derby.
At night my father read books –
books by foreign authors. Books on horticulture.
I missed my mother, her bossomy richness,

the stink of her Raleigh straights. But she never showed up
in Haggard. We got a letter from back in Derby.
(By then my father'd begun his detonations.)
After sunset my father took me to the swamp

and showed me the boxes in his flatbed.
He had me count them, check them off, then to scare me,
he opened one, shined his flashlight in and I
pretended not to look. We had an agreement

that I'd tell no one, not even Mother. The two of us sat
over cold cups of tea, the fireplace crackling, the boxes
humming in that raw darkness & my father said
what he was doing was sacred, sacred.

II.

CASTAWAYS

Five of us – me plus Uncle Dave,
my old man & Bryce, father of Bryce Jr.,
a leaky fishing boat & a border collie
named Shep, glued together in some

blood & bullshit mix – slipped
through the Halifax fog, unlabeled whisky
in the hold, stashed crates of
tinned tuna on its way to Down East Maine.

I was fourteen then, stowed among
the scallop nets, the stinking scuppers,
dreaming a girl I'd met two years before:
Hello, Ellie said, I'm Ellie. Skinny,

Pony tailed kid, a year older than me,
riding her mother's roan mare on the headland
above Hatch's Cove. I watched her come
and fade away, legs bouncing, the clanking

blueberry buckets; I'd keep that thought
those seasick days – how on Ellie's porch,
I felt beneath her dress while the Kelvinator
hummed. Her voice was a low murmur,

little puffs of breath. Ellie & I'd drive down
to Derby, she at the wheel of the red Rambler –
miles of hackmatack, a blaze of fireweed
under a New Brunswick sky –

and roll past the hockey stick factory
to the A-frame Uncle Dave built
in '69, looking for my swashbuckling
uncle & my father. Mom wants you back,

I said to no one I could name: they'd
cleared out two days before & Ellie
and I snooped in the random clutter; a note –
"gone fishing" – was pinned to the bathroom

door. We sat outside & ate our sandwiches
& I said I loved her; maybe you do,
she said, her breath hard against my chest;
then, after a minute, she asked what that

had to do with my father's leaving us –
my mother, my big brother Chet; scrunched
in a sleeping bag, we gazed at the August
stars & she kissed me while the future

flooded in. She kissed me. Let me
tell you about Ellie's body, the way
her rib cage rose & fell when I touched
her hips. Morning, a jay's shrill cry woke us –

a blue flicker in the choke cherries – and Ellie
turned to me, her hair dew-slick, the day
unfolding, as it always did. I said we'd
drive south to Haggard where my old man

& Uncle Dave holed up for week-long drunks.
So we're on Lake Hazard, water dark
& roily, waves slapping the snooty prow
of a leaky skiff. Haggard's no more than

a potato field, deerflies pestering
an Esso Pump where duck hunters tank up.
Up ahead we see those decoys – evening
greens, autumn reds riding the oily

swell, and Uncle Dave fires a warning shot
across our bow: apologies all
around, and my Dad offers a toast to me
and Ellie, to Mom, his "water widow"

back in Pubnico. Of course it's empty ritual.
The duck dinner. The gooseberry pie.

Even my father's erstwhile affection
is a way to flirt with Ellie who's high

on Uncle Dave's apple wine. That's how I
remember it – the early Fall chill,
a fire's crackle, the gamey taste of
Merganser duck. The marsh asleep around us.

The muddled dark. Then I scoop up Ellie
in my arms, lug her to the skiff and slip into
the moonlit lake, leaving Dad & Uncle Dave
asleep & drunk. I did all this –

a kid of fifteen, did my solemn son's
duty & was done. The highway led straight back
via Ellie's Aunt Mim's house in Frederickton
to Halifax. I slept on Mim's smoking couch,

woke early to crowing banties & Mim's
plinking piano. Ellie scootched onto
the pillows – we fucked to those cock
a-doodles & scherzos: I remember

the look on Ellie's face, her wide-eyed
grin – we did it again & again, a
near-defunct spinet slipping into
the theme from Brigadoon, brandy snifters

splinking in Mim's sky-blue pie safe, rain
beating the panes, a maritime rain
glazing Mim's perky hollyhocks & mums,
and we breakfasted on kippers & scones

and the scent of Ellie's sex mingled
with the gentle September rain. She
wanted to stay put in Frederickton –
we began eleventh grade there & were both

happy. Rain scudded the lawn & garden a sweet
lavender-gray, Mim's piano students' wet
galoshes lined up like rubber duckies
in the hall, and Ellie, accompanied

by Mim, began to sing afternoons,
Rogers and Hart, Cole Porter, Lerner and Lowe –
& I'd sit in the bay window, looking out
at the happy rain. My father & Uncle Dave

returned to Halifax – my mother phoned
to say my uncle had put a bullet
in his head, and I felt nothing but numb,
Uncle Dave dead, my mother shucking clams

at the Dockside, my father on
a nonstop spree. He's got the shakes now,
Uncle Dave's buried in the cherry orchard
overlooking our drowsy little town,

my mother said. Ellie and I stayed into
the nor'easters of November;
Mim bought Ellie new skirts, jewelry, blouses –
& in December Ellie took

the star role in *Annie Get Your Gun* –
a feisty, dirty-blonde Annie, she
brought down the Acadian Opera house with
"I Can Do Anything Better than You Can."

The three of us, Aunt Mim, Ellie, me
had a cast party Christmas night where
Mim banged out "I'll be Seeing You" ("in all
those old familiar places. . .") & Ellie

sang the lyrics & the tears came to Mim's eyes:
fumbling for her hanky, she murmurs, "Sing it
again, again." Knowing we'd leave next day,
that we had to leave – Ellie was even more

teary-eyed – we sat in the kitchen's dark
sipping Cutty Sark from jelly jar glasses,
& savored the blue tree lights, the window creche
with its ceramic Christ child, the assembled wise men

with sheep & angels. I don't know when
it came to me we'd do this again,
but I saw in Mim's cracked China face a map
of the world, the latitudinally

creased forehead & eyebrows, her chin's deep-
cleft meridian. Sail away, Mim cried,
sail away! Boxing Day morning Ellie
& I squeeze into the red Rambler

& head northeast across the Nova Scotia
border, snow doffing the salt box houses
huddled against the storm; snow on the rude
stone churches, scribbled into the aftertaste

of Mim's tart plum pudding, a swirl
of crumpled lights, passing semis, rigs
gone off the erased road. Ellie drives.
Snow above our hubcaps, the gas gauge

reads empty; the Rambler stops beneath icy
alders – & a moment goes by, it all seems
seared clean – even the spruce bows stop
swaying. I'd like to say this portends

things to come, that somehow it implies
Ellie, me, our linked trajectory,
but up ahead paths diverge – years spin out,
one after another. The last eclipse

I saw when I was eleven killed bees,
turned goat's milk sour. In this stilled moment,
it seems, our arctic sun converges
with an arctic moon, snowflakes float suspended.

And so, at the edge of childhood, peering
out the frosty rear window, we see the shades,
the half shapes of bad timing, botched karma.
"I don't believe in fate," Ellie says. "Do you?"

"I can't say," I say. What I'm afraid to say
– can't know – is we're bound together,

Ellie and I, & in the blistering cold
we hold each other, won't let go.

An hour later, we drag our frosty butts
into Roonie's Body Parts. It's Boxing Day.
Roonie glances from a salt encrusted
Pinto's guts, her smile flickers –

a cigar smolders in the pit. For pinups,
Roonie's pasted glossies of autographed
movie stars – Heston, Brando, Cagney –
along the dusty walls & musty cornices.

A dank stench, a soppy thickness in here –
& Roonie, all five cute skinny feet
of her, dances from tool box to oil pan,
bolts rattling, keys jingling on her belt,

& announces – more to an ancient black lab
dozing in the dark than us – she'll supply lunch
if we help pull out the Pinto's dead engine
cradled above the pit, but Roonie winches

it herself: we breathe in the reek of
motor oil & stogies; we shiver
in the damp; outside snow hazes a wasteland
of stripped chassis, a rusty derrick.

Roonie's father had on his deathbed bequeathed
the shop to Roonie & a diabetic
brother; over barley soup she tells us
how when her brother passed away she quit

her daycare job to pump gas. I keep the province going,
she quips to Ellie. (She's half asleep.)
Around her pin-neat flat there's photos
of her dead family – dead mother & brother,

both sadly, palely, fat, her father
in mounted snapshots on what look like
tundra fishing trips. A stuffed cod (or scrod)
swims above the mantle. Tiny plaster

sea captains do a hornpipe accompanied
by clucking cuckoo clocks, automated angels.
"Sometimes I'd like to sail far away from this,"
Roonie shrugs – & that phrase, "Sail away,"

snags on Mim's last goodbyes. Two weeks later,
we're still rooming at Roonie's Gas & Oil.
Ellie's learned the nuts & bolts of transmissions,
the trigonometries of spark & ignition

while I spend my idle time reading Roonie's
sailing books: Dana's "Two Years Before the Mast,"
Slocum's – "Sailing Around the World Alone,"
& the January snow pelts down.

One Saturday Roonie dons plaid kilts, warms up
a wheezing bag pipe & we're off to the grange dance
in Calabash, the little Scots town:
this romance – the three of us whirling

to fifes & drums, high stepping higher,
higher to a Gallic chant that thrums
our hearts & tosses us reeling into
an evening snow where gauzy streetlights

gush onto ruddy-faced dancers.
Oh, Happy time! Happy, happy time!
– inseparable the three of us –
you know it can't last. But we keep up

the madly rushing dance till morning,
kilts flying, bodies throbbing to a honk
& hum that pounds our heads, sends us to bed
dizzy with the "bagpipe bends." The cold

seeps around doorstops, seizes engine blocks,
the cold – enemy of faith, hammer of
Godless want: at forty below, smoke droops beneath
chimney pots, the sun implodes. A drone of skidoos,

the snap of maples, breaks the silence.
Look: a crescent moon curls above Ellie's

head. She dreams a fish & chips joint in Halifax,
steam boiling from greasy vats. Her mother works

the night shift serving stinky wharf rats.
When she wakes, she cries to Roonie & me,
"Anything but that," though she knows the past
looms – nothing changes – still it's snowing,

still January: day after day's
punctuated by turnip soup, boiled
cabbages. When Roonie comes down with flu,
Ellie puts on her grease-monkey suit,

changes oil, tunes up Calabash's crates
& junk heaps; she's learned the ins & outs
of carburetors & differentials,
knows the stalled stillness of cracked engine blocks;

and in the dusky quiet she putters
till Roonie's flu becomes pneumonia,
& old Doc Gregory – a bespectacled
Scots homeopath – prescribes crackpot tonics,

and cryptically calls Roonie's fever
the "buddy's wee try to cure itself;"
so the air in Roonie's room buzzes –
a choir, an angelic chorus sings

with such cherubic sweetness Roonie swoons,
cries out for rye (not scotch); slugging down
a shot glass, she revives – . Ellie & I watch
the room fill with blue transparent wings;

our patient's face bursts into a smile
of such warmth & gentleness – such sweetness –
we're stunned to silence. Barely fifteen, sixteen,
our lives just starting, yet half over,

& I'm too young to be a saint – so's Roonie.
Out in the blizzard night, as snow wafts over me,
through frosty windows I see hazy half shapes,
guttering candles – and it comes to me

I've never asked myself if I believe in God,
never mind if there *is* a God,
and I never looked inside, didn't ask,
couldn't bear it – & so when the question comes

I'm edgy, cynical. Should I care,
what's in it for me, God or no God?
I walk a mile to the snoozing village.
past the Saints of Acadia Church's tinseled

stain glass windows' baptism scenes
& stark north country miracles,
and it comes to me the God I should
believe in isn't the hoary-bearded God

I believed in who rules these pages. . .

At Lyme

David got a job in Lyme at the dog track
injecting the wippets with speed. We took one home
that was all used up – it had something like rickets,
legs splayed out, kidneys almost gone.
A sweet little Snoopy, but she loved to run. Had to run.
In her last blue light, she was David's Dahlia.
He called her the Hound of Heaven. I like to think of her, jaunty & flirty,
a dog that was all girl. But when we left Lyme,
David said we had to shoot her. We rode out
to the dump, Dahlia between him & me,
but David couldn't – wouldn't – & the truth is,
I was the cold-hearted one. (I'd learned from drowning kittens.)

I walked her past the ratty packing crates,
the dead refrigerators, to the landfill's edge
where, as the Penobscot oxbows, one part's
brisk & flowing, the other sluiced into weedy pools.
Dumps can be pleasant places –
nothing says a dump needs to be anything
but what it is – and a dog finds lots to inspect,
as Dahlia did: I would like to say I found a suitcase
full of money in the Lyme dump; that the Lord
found it within Himself to intervene before
I put a bullet in Dahlia's head. Nuts
to those who think it's anyone but us
who make the big decisions.

At Biff's Donuts,

Everybody's putting everybody down –
blab this, blab that. Halifax is alive with users & Biff's
a fire trap. I wanted out even before

my old friend David – who I'm conveniently
in love with – asked me to sail south
on a leaky boat he inherited from his recently

deceased uncle. Not that I don't have
reasons for moving, one being I'm pregnant; the other
that I'm haunted by the ghost of Biff,

who died last winter (an overdose of perogoric).
He returns nights (I work the night shift)
to inspect the place: he's given up

trying to convert me to his Fundamentalist faith,
but said I still had a chance to quit
whatever I'd done to provoke my condition.

One morning I saw the Great Hawk Migration.
I saw a turtle hatch – scores of them
crawling down the embankment to Biff's

Pond. I stood outside, amazed at Nature
& when David's truck pulled up Biff's spirit
hovered around us as we drove off,

a little puddle of Biff-light (no, it wasn't
shaped like a donut). He's the devil of
past delights – you don't need that kind

of devil, my David said as I lay back
in the big tub where he was washing my neck.
I kissed his sweetsmelling chest –

and we made a sudsy love while Biff's puff
of ectoplasmic light bounced against the window.

Pastoral

Later, mushroom picking
we come on two deer fucking –
antlered stag
& pitiful doe in the high
wheatcolored grass.

Local Color

Riding along the town's murky margins,
bank clock ticking, the Dairy Freeze

locked in dreariness, ROUTE 105
slimy as a calf's tongue,

and my radio's purling the callers'
names – Carlo, Wayne, Rosetta – as each

three-AM voice bursts beyond
this bare road, these headlights, the highway

clicking, the Halifax lights not far off.
I am sober for once in my life but

grateful, astonished, I'm pulled over.
I believe in forgiveness and restitution, in

Karma and Payback, in Justification
and Remorse, I say to Dale, the Deputy

Sheriff. Just step out of your car, sir,
step lightly, he says, and I am less

than delighted. I'm slurry with sleep.
The windshield's blurry: the cop's tart

voice snaps me awake; the handcuffs –
the handcuffs he clamps

on my wrists are luminous. Slumped
in the back of Dale's cruiser,

I hear the call go in – I watch the dials
On his dash go dim.

There's the odor of riverbank
and filthy collars, the sheriff's

manic breath flooding the cruiser
like jacklight. Dale slips into the street,

eyes catching my aboriginal plate:
it's my wife's illegal car and Dale's

inscrutable, "They should've thrown him
in a ditch; dogs in our town,

they're treated better than this,"
makes my teeth chatter. Hazed

in honeyed northern light, in
this scintillant strobe-lit

moment, the backup cop,
guy named Jim (Slim CITGO Jim)

identifies me as nonIndian,
just one more fuckedup . . . white

fuckup. . . , tawny
gaze drifting to Dale

whose twin exhausts sputter
beyond Dale's cruiser

into the Micmac night.
Jim fingers me as the "old man"

of an Indian. But he ain't drunk,
Dale says. Besides, lies Jim,

can't give him a breath
check if we got no breath-a-lyzer,

and I'm out on the highway
and the broken yellow line splits into

halves & quarters. Halfway
down the road I mumble what I recall of

a white man's prayer. I lean into a
solar wind smelling of wildflowers

that used to grow here, chamomille,
Indian paintbrush, daisies, butterwort.

They fold, infold, along
a littered berm, wilt & bloom under

a thicket of stars white as Queen Anne's lace.

Reach

Days after my father's burial I'd sold his place near Pubnico
& moved out of the White Horse Laundry, bought a new boat
and made up with Ellie. During a break of sunny weather,
we sailed down a placid Bay of Fundy to Maine.
Ellie was seven months pregnant (another man, another time)
and we drifted easy among the islands, fishing a little.
One night off a cove where at sunset you could see the pale shapes
of deer come out to lick the salt, Ellie said she thought
I'd changed since my mother died; for the kind of guy I was,
I'd changed, she said. I slapped a mosquito on her arm:
a needlemark of blood leaked out and I kissed it;
Ellie pressed her belly next to mine. Truth is I was thinking
about how my mother died, *her* way of dying, all the way
from Nova Scotia. Deep in her quilt, she faced the early
traffic and in that silence, she watched her life roll by.
I'd spend the last week holding Mom's hand, for the first time
in her life while I talked she'd listen: I'd talk about childhood,
about what she'd taught me – those little bits of maternal wisdom –
and this, I think, quieted her somewhat. When that deathbed
atmosphere got too much, I'd go walking, and that's when she died –
no-one, not even the night nurse was there. Each time
I'd pick up the phone to call the funeral home, I'd break down –
and so: my mother's bedside, her last night, nothing but
the peeper's going at it and her body turning cold beside me.
I stopped there – Ellie wanted me to go on, but I couldn't.
I felt the baby turn & the tide pull at the mooring; but, even then
who knows if what I felt for my mother wasn't love but a kind of pity –
or sorrow, Ellie said. Next morning the wind was up & we headed
down Eggemoggin Reach past Deer Isle, the sails double reefed,
the cockpit zipped up, sweet Ellie retching over the side.

Dockside

I went back to the Dockside when David
was ten. At that time Brendan began his
Cuban transactions, 1975– .

David liked two things: boats & books. He took
after his father – a loner. Got his
sweet nature, his saint-like temper, from me his mother.

But he'd do anything for Brendan –
draw pictures of the old man in a mustache
& seedy vest. Brendan would disappear

weeks at a time, return with wads
of worthless foreign money. My son
couldn't get enough of him, though Brendan

hardly knew David slept under the same roof.
For a while we had money & I quit
the Dockside, helped Brendan bottle his homemade

schnapps when he wasn't carting cigarettes
down to Maine. Then Brendan & David went south
to Haggard across the line from Derby.

I returned to the Dockside. I got sad frantic
letters from my son (who hated his
vagabondage) & I became one of those

ladies you read about in novels,
cultivated, but condemned to a peasant's
life; God knows, I deserved more than this,

doesn't everybody? On my deathbed,
my son returned home without his father.
I never learned how Brendan died, but I

met him a few years later in the Kiln
of the Second Order. My job was to wet
down the bodies – a job like any other,

no worse than my hell-on-earth factory job:
there's no justice on this side of mortality's
dividing line, I told Brendan, though

as a dead man he heard me less than he'd have alive.

Hunger

Often sometimes
in the morning at the
sun porch table.
The bay below & noisy rocks.
Or walking back
from the outpatient clinic,
fingering the sutures,
I wondered if
she waited for me,
& a stillness
would come over
the land & water,
& though I was dogtired,
I'd climb the walls
of the old fort
& look out over the cove
into the bay
& think of the currents
through which my love
ran for her,
& I'd scour my mind
for the things I thought
still held her to me:
a ragged white dress,
brass hairpin
& the table
would be laid –
boiled eggs, a sliver
of ocean-green lime.
She'd eat while
I was watching her.
She'd sit on the
edge of the Pubnico dock
feet kicking the water,
rolling a smoke,
squinty

from the sun's
glaze – & then
she'd disappear
over the side –
splash, brief ripples. Gone.
Cigarette still smoldering on deck.
And I'd look
out to see her surface,
the water dimpling
her back –
those little naked wings –
& I'd watch her swim,
her underwater glide,
& she'd surface
a moment. I never knew
who she'd be
when she came up –
but I tell you
I was blessed those days,
I was hungry
& didn't even know it.
When we first met I'd sit
down to clams
piled high, flounder sizzling,
fries & scallops
mounded on my plate
& because I didn't
eat, I began to have a look of
an unfed animal.
You'd think she'd have
fattened me up
– she liked me all ribs,
I was like the lines
in a skinny poem.
And she
became my ideal,
this woman
I'd been in love with once
who'd been lost
to me all those years. This
was serious: I began

to think about
what I might eat.

PORTRAIT

Before I left Biff, I asked him
if he could paint a picture of my baby's
guardian angel. Do it for me,
I said, redeem yourself, Biff –
and in hours he'd done more than that.
After the baby was born & died, I began to look for signs
in the coffee grinds, I watched for them
in the sad little mums. I watched the wrinkled face
of my baby's angel turn an ungodly blue.
Meanwhile the portrait just hung there,
and I remembered how Biff had said,
Come here, you won't get pregnant, how he
said it something like that.
Then I knew I was. And I didn't get dreamy,
didn't puke my eyes out, didn't.

Ferris' Wheel of History

I remember this two-thousand
miles from Halifax, Ellie sick again,
the Bryce tied to the Key West
dock. A few old salts – retirees

in polyesters – look at me funny.
We're both down with heatstroke. Near broke.
The boat leaks. So when Ellie says, tell a story,
I fish around in an old tackle box

to find that daguerreotype of great granddad
Ferris fresh off the boat, bulbous nose,
straight quarrelsome lips. And another
of a well-established Ferris dressed

to the nines on a dappled horse. He's history:
I was in history class the first & last year
I went to college, hunched over my mid-
term essay on my Irish relatives;

I tell Ellie I'm an imposter, too:
how can she believe a half-Irish past
a college kid feeds to his Provincial
History prof? As a kid, I write,

I learned to hate Indians – I'm part
Micmac, same as killed great-grandfather
Ferris three years after he sailed
from Dublin and not before he married

my great-grandmother & fathered Granddad.
Tweed was Ferris' business – fact is
I can't remember if it was tweed
or woolens. He sold bolts of Irish tweed,

I write. He'd also got a grain concession

and shipped millet & hops North where
everyone knew that brand, Ferris Tweed, & still starved.
But I never knew him, I write, nor did

my grandfather who was three when Ferris,
blind drunk, toppled from the bridge
of a tuna schooner. Imagine him
a no-nonsense man, filled with boozy

self-importance – a slice of Irish
arrogance gone to the Grand Banks' bottom.
It takes all kinds, I wrote, but sometimes
I wish I hadn't heard my father tell it:

"'. . . an Indian named Jenks pushed
your great granddad into the drink,'"
I wrote, and a haunted Jenks rose
before my eyes, the room swam; then I was

ten years older, looking past the wharf
to a sleek pink houseboat: a radio
crackles; ice cubes tinkle in a glass.
Ellie's brown body's crimsoned by the

outline of our mast & halyards.
When I left the classroom – the last to leave –
in spotty October sunlight (I tell
Ellie) I had a revelation

that my father's story of Ferris'
untimely death was a way of warning me
of a nasty family trait: but you're
no imposter, Ellie says; her belly

has creases in it from where she lay
face down on the deck (the bay's baked
sea-green) & Father's oceanic voice rises
& falls with the cadence of the Atlantic.

My father – no doubt drunk --
made it all up, I say. But there's
that dirty little photograph of Ferris

dressed in his dandy Irish; there's

this college kid in his last semester
at Dalhousie U. trying to impress upon his prof
his story is more than pumped-up facts.
I drank an ale at a college bar –

& four drafts later, called my father
who lived a pauper's life in Pubnico,
told him how I wrote Ferris'
story – & was it true? I asked. What the fuck

is true said my father. I heard him fumble
for a match & then he coughed his awful cough:
Ferris was a drunk & a son-of-a-bitch
like you, he said. Hack-hack. And hung up.

I've fixed Ellie dinner – more conch & fries.
She's lost my story's thread but
blinks herself awake; true to me –
to my father, a decade dead –- I pour

a drink and glance up at Ellie &
to the Gulf Stream stars; I think about
him stuck in Pubnico, the autumn
storms closing in. I'd left Dalhousie

for a gas-pumping job; and as for Ferris,
I tell Ellie, maybe he never lived. . . maybe he went
through an imposter's motions, but like the rest
of us knew his real vice was melancholy –

The Unpardonable Sin, Ellie says,
a phrase I haven't heard since Bible Camp;
she hoists herself into the cockpit,
begins washing out her frayed undies,

hangs them on a trellis of ropes & stays,
then gives me a weak grin just as a
rum Florida moon rises over
the marina's skeletal mastheads.

Still Life

I knocked and entered the yellow house,
greeted by a shock of

staggered papers
cut by gray window light

and the Danish Symphony

louder than I thought
anyone could stand it,

him in a straightbacked chair
in a shadowed corner

of a room adjacent to the entryway
framed by two windows from which

my octogenarian prof peered without
being seen.

In his seclusion, he seemed even
more like

my concept of
an aging Goethe, having
the right furniture, the *imprimatur*

of a wise and rancorous old man,

except I knew
what outweighed the wisdom,

and that he'd arranged this "sitting"
so when I saw him – heard the
oceanic music – I'd feel as though

I'd stumbled onto something resembling a ruin.

Doomed Love

I took to them right off, Ellie & her big slow eyes
& David with a grin that was meant for her
but lit up everything. Neither seemed to know
how when the wind kicks up, instinct
(which David had) without knowledge
(a doubtful quantity) can tear your
heart out. Ellie and David
anchored their sloop outside the marina:
headed down to Cuba – a sentimental, a political voyage,
David said, though neither he nor his woman seemed
the type; in their little galley
she deep-fried a conch; there were pictures
of Maine & Nova Scotia pasted on the bulkhead.
The "Bryce" was neatly shipshape:
its appointments polished beyond brightness. An habitation
of the newly infatuated. I drove home.
I wanted to go back – to be around a love that,
knowing them only a couple of hours,
I knew was an errant & doomed love.

Turtle

So I should sit down,
sit down, David said, you've
got sunstroke. I did and inside my head

was a little a hall of mirrors.
The boat knocking against its painter,
the sea grass whooshing.

The wind dropped, the reef fish rose
In our wake. I looked at David.
I wanted to squeeze him half to death,

I was *that* crazy. And I fell asleep.
Come to me, my sweet turtle!
I found myself saying.

A sea turtle. I'd stumbled on one
pawing its way to the water –
round-backed, nasty bird snout,

you could almost see it breathe,
& behind it washes of sea light
& the shadows of our bodies. He's

still there, David said. *She*,
I said. There's a difference.
Crunching to the half moon bay,

afraid like everything out here
on the last stretch of beach is afraid.
But turtle goes no place, just eats

so much before she crowds herself out.
I wake & hold my lover: I climb
out of my body. That's what the sun does

to you, dear turtle. Slow eyes.
Something like a grin. But
she can't hear me now.

Sanctuary

A monk's garden walkway;
broken windows – scent of limes,
empty, save for the occasional

dragonfly. The rain had stopped:
I sat down & loved the simplicity
of just giving out to my Lord,

not having my say. A kind of weed
grew up, a green tangle,
& palmettos in their springtime

lushness. From the empty
ruin of a kitchen, even more quiet:
so I stayed an hour, smoking, not thinking.

Dominican, Franciscan –
what was it? At the hour
my soul flew into the darkness,

a dragonfly glided over
the crumbling garden wall.
Without warning night fell; I saw

through a break in the foliage
the town folded into itself. Up
in the scoured mountains

rose the moon, sweet & wild.

Aubade

Her last letter
lies beside the window,
the morning light
slanting across it. She
says she misses the garden,
the tired house in Lyme
but can't come back.
The jays battle with her
here or not, a squall of feathers
above the white yard.
At noon the snow begins
in earnest. I see the ghost
of her move downhill
to the sleeping village,
the snow heavy alongside
the road. She stands in a
crosswind and enters
a kind of rapt
silence. Only the late-
winter snow, the direction-
less shift of color
from brown and dull red,
a crow color. Across
lengthened rows of field
and scrub growth
winter returns, stiffened,
layering down. The mountains
are terrifying and tumble
behind her with a final coldness.

The Winter Journal

You wake, my dear Peggy,

to the mantle clock ticking quietly –
it too is afraid of the future –

and the cat looks up from her chair,
dewy eyed,
as the words rise into

the musty air.

An empty book's
sprawled on a table. Its pages

(scribbled, then tossed away)

empty cogitations
in which our protagonist

rubs his eyes
after each note taken

and stares out at an unlikely
patch of grass.

        All thread
of narrative

is blurred by what
you can't see in the distance:

you
pause

over a story so simple it can be wrapped in
a pine nut, an acorn –

her car swerving to avoid a pedestrian,
the surgeon dropping his scalpel

in mid-incision.

Neither the hungry voices of the poor nor an angry wind

can be heard. And so is heard

        an indecency exposed

after the first storm arrives

and March light
drains the words from

our protagonist's journal.

A thought begins, then is broken

(Who, my dear, will interrogate who?)

and all but abandoned the winter journal
cannot write itself;

its ideas
are torn from the cold ground,

bald roots

planted
in another hard season.

Acknowledgments

Some of these poems appeared, in slightly different form, in H*ayden's Ferry Review*, *Gathering of the Tribes*, *Great River Review*, *Literary Review*, *Manhattan Review*, *Passages North*, *Texas Review*, *Whisky Island* and elsewhere.

Grateful thanks to the hugely talented Morgan O'Connell for her beautiful paintings. She saw what I was after. And to Donna Bister and Marc Estrin for their encouragement and creative insight, and to whatever muse blew in and out of my life, delivering these strange poems. And, always, to Suzanne.

—Tony Whedon

Many thanks to Tony for his unwavering support and to Donna and Marc for providing me with the humbling opportunity to be a part of such an amazing collaboration.

—Morgan O'Connell

Fomite

A fomite is a medium capable of transmitting infectious organisms from one individual to another.

"The activity of art is based on the capacity of people to be infected by the feelings of others." Tolstoy, *What Is Art?*

Writing a review on Amazon, Good Reads, Shelfari, Library Thing or other social media sites for readers will help the progress of independent publishing. To submit a review, go to the book page on any of the sites and follow the links for reviews. Books from independent presses rely on reader to reader communications.

Visit http://www.fomitepress.com/FOMITE/Our_Books.html for more information or to order any of our books.

As It Is On Earth
Peter M Wheelwright

Dons of Time
Greg Guma

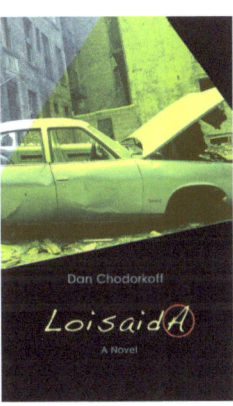
Loisaida
Dan Chodorkoff

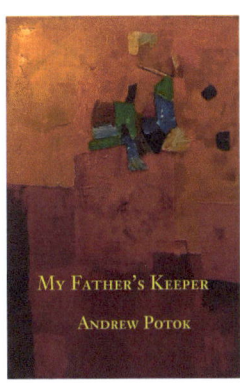
My Father's Keeper
Andrew Potok

My God, What Have We Done
Susan V Weiss

Rafi's World
Fred Russell

Fomite

The Co-Conspirator's Tale
Ron Jacobs

Short Order Frame Up
Ron Jacobs

All the Sinners Saints
Ron Jacobs

Travers' Inferno
L. E. Smith

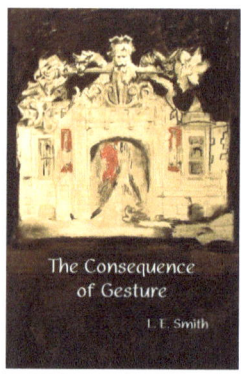
The Consequence of Gesture
L. E. Smith

Raven or Crow
Joshua Amses

Sinfonia Bulgarica
Zdravka Evtimova

The Good Muslim
of Jackson Heights
Jaysinh Birjépatil

The Moment Before an Injury
Joshua Amses

Fomite

The Return of
Jason Green
Suzi Wizowaty

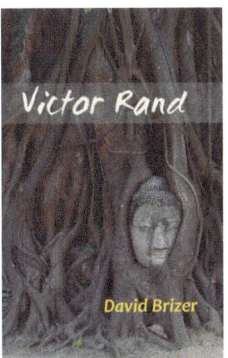
Victor Rand
David Brizeri

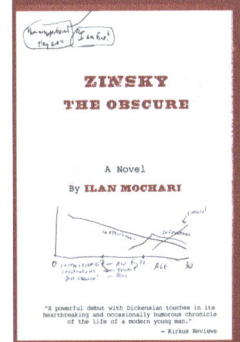
Zinsky the Obscure
Ilan Mochari

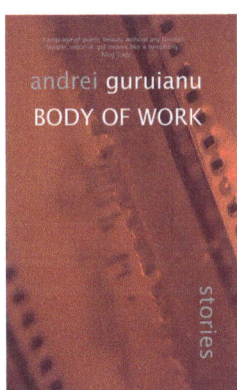
Body of Work
Andrei Guruianu

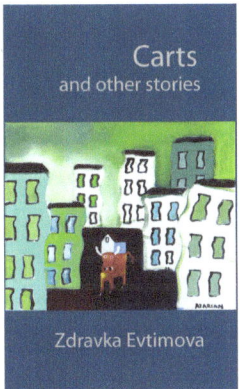
Carts and Other Stories
Zdravka Evtimova

Flight
Jay Boyer

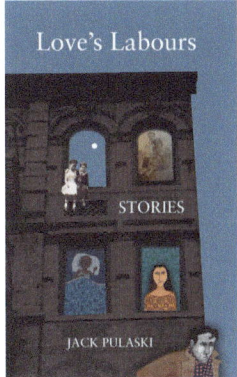
Love's Labours
Jack Pulaski

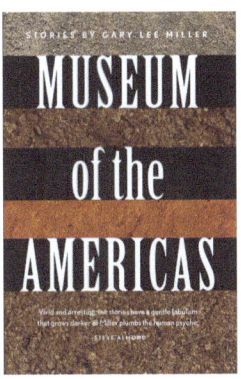
Museum of the Americas
Gary Lee Miller

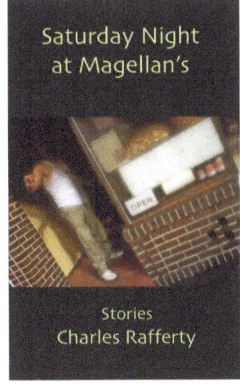
Saturday Night at Magellan's
Charles Rafferty

Fomite

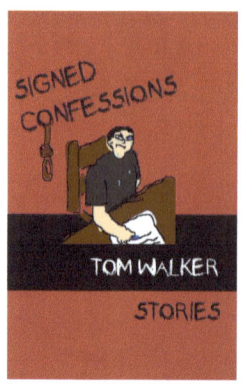
Signed Confessions
Tom Walker

Still Time
Michael Cocchiarale

Suite for Three Voices
Derek Furr

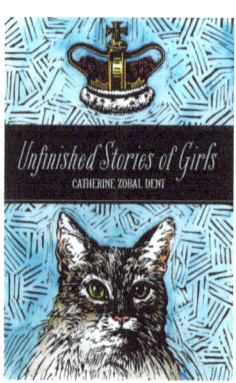
Unfinished Stories of Girls
Catherine Zobal Dent

Views Cost Extra
L. E. Smith

Visiting Hours
Jennifer Anne Moses

When You Remeber
Deir Yassin
R. L. Green

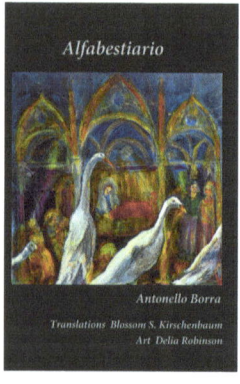
Alfabestiaro
Antonello Borra

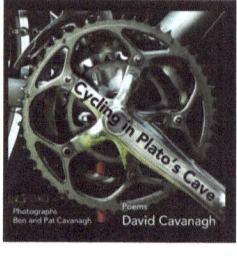
Cycling in Plato's Cave
David Cavanagh

Fomite

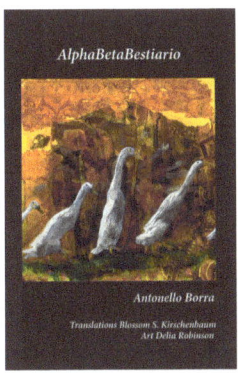
AlphaBetaBestiario
Antonello Borra

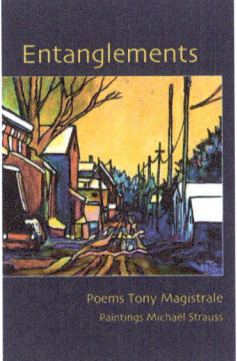
Entanglements
Tony Magistrale

Everyone Lives Here
Sharon Webster

Four-Way Stop
Sherry Olson

Improvisational Arguments
Anna Faktorovitch

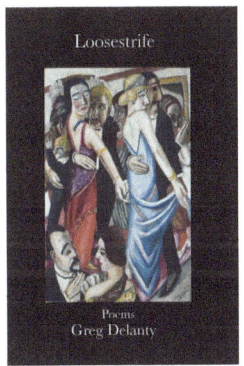
Loosestrife
Greg Delanty

Meanwell
Janice Miller Potter

Roadworthy Creature
Roadworth Craft
Kate Magill

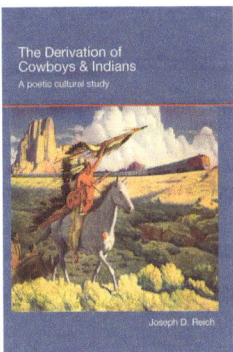
The Derivation of
Cowboys & Indians
Joseph D. Reich

Fomite

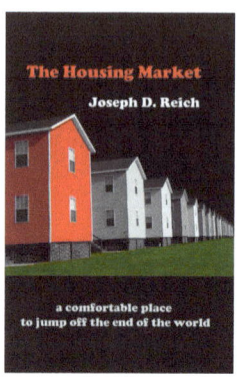
The Housing Market
Joseph D. Reich

The Empty Notebook
Interrogates Itself
Susan Thomas

The Hundred Yard
Dash Man
Barry Goldensohn

The Listener Aspires
to the Condition of Music
Barry Goldensohn

The Way None
of This Happened
Mike Breiner

Screwed
Stephen Goldberg

Planet Kasper
Peter Schumann

My Murder
and Other Local News
David Schein

Picking Up the Bodies
James F. Connolly

www.ingramcontent.com/pod-product-compliance
Lightning Source LLC
Chambersburg PA
CBHW040202100526
44592CB00001B/9